LOOKING BACK

LOOKING BACK

Images of New England
1860-1930

Selected and Edited by Susan Mahnke

Yankee Publishing Incorporated   Dublin, New Hampshire

Contents

Book and jacket design by Guy Russell

Yankee Publishing Incorporated
Dublin, New Hampshire 03444

First Edition

Copyright 1982, by Yankee Publishing Incorporated
Printed in the United States of America

Library of Congress Catalog Card No. 82-60272
ISBN: 0-911658-37-8

Introduction

You don't need to be old yourself, or a photographer, an historian, or even a New Englander to enjoy looking at old photographs of New England. The fascination with these images seems to transcend generations, and geography, and other things that divide people. Old photographs unite us with a moment, a place, a person in the past. They tell us where we have been (which, as we say in New England, we need to know before we can tell where we're going!). Old photographs make us wonder. Did the little girl on page 55 always vividly remember the day she saw the wrecked ship on a Nantucket beach — or is it we who are haunted by Baldwin Coolidge's image of that scene?

The photographs in this book were taken by twelve photographers (nine men and three women) — some professional, some amateur — who used their cameras to record life in New England, and used New England to anchor their subjects to a place. Some, like Henry Peabody (in love with travel) or the cool professional Baldwin Coolidge, ranged all over New England, often making the landscape their subject. Others, including George Tingley and Lena Osgood Long, never went more than a few miles from their homes but still found rich supplies of photographic subjects. Their motivations for using the awkward tripod camera and heavy glass negatives of the day ranged from the purely esthetic (Emma Lewis Coleman's moody photographs that emulated the Barbizon school of French painting) and the purely personal (Frederick Greene's fond record of family life and Henry Hadcock's storefront scenes in his Roxbury, Massachusetts, neighborhood) to recreational (Warwick Stevens Carpenter's carefree candids of outings with his college friends) and photojournalistic (newspaper reporter Wilfred Stone's record of community life in Cranston, Rhode Island, and Henry Moore's rare prints of the Third New Hampshire Regiment in the Civil War).

Fred Quimby's photographs were part family album, part business, for he sold at his studio the scenes of coastal Maine farm life that starred his own family. Chansonetta Stanley Emmons went them all one better: she used her camera to record not what existed at the moment, but what had been. She often painstakingly costumed and composed her neighbors near Kingfield, Maine, to create photographs that idealized an earlier era and conveyed a nostalgia, as writer Brendan Gill put it, "not only for what used to be, but for what ought to have been."

Old photographs are sometimes found today in unexpected places, and the pictures in this book are no exception. Only hours before they were to be auctioned off, Lena Osgood Long's photographs were rescued from an attic by the president of a local historical society who had the presence of mind to realize the value of her find. Warwick Stevens Carpenter's glass negatives were found in an old summer camp that had been unvisited for years. A new cache of Fred Quimby's glass negatives, including the touching and unusual scene on page 63, turned up just this year (along with the realization that Fred Quimby's uncle, George Henry Donnell, whom Mr. Quimby frequently photographed, was also a favorite model of Emma Coleman when she was in York, Maine). In several cases, most notably those of George Tingley and Wilfred Stone, descendants of the photographers had taken excellent care of the work, certain that someday someone would come along and appreciate the photographs. And in many instances, knowledgeable archivists like Ellie Reichlin at the Society for the Preservation of New England Antiquities in Boston and William Copely at the New Hampshire Historical Society in Concord knew exactly where to turn when someone came in looking for little-known collections by individual photographers.

Whenever possible, original prints have been used to keep the reproductions as faithful as possible. All of the Lena Osgood Long photographs, and many of the George Tingley and Chansonetta Stanley Emmons photographs, were printed by the photographer. In other cases the original negatives (those old glass plates are less fragile than one would think) had survived and new prints could be made from them. Most are published here for the first time — creating a family album for New Englanders, and for people everywhere.

Henry Peabody with his photographic equipment,
probably during the 1940s.

Henry Greenwood Peabody

Henry Greenwood Peabody, son of the Reverend Charles and Henrietta (Greenwood) Peabody, was born in St. Louis, Missouri, in 1855, and attended schools there and in Pennsylvania to prepare for college. In 1872 his father, an alumnus of Dartmouth College (Class of 1839), sent his son east to matriculate at the same school in Hanover, New Hampshire. While at Dartmouth Henry Peabody discovered an aptitude for photography, which he took up in his senior year, and a love for the New England landscape.

Although he continued to study photography as an avocation, Henry Peabody's life for the ten years after graduation followed the standard course of graduate study in electricity and architecture, work as an electrical engineer in Chicago, and marriage (to Dora C. Phelps of Evanston, Illinois). But his attraction to New England and fascination with photography proved overwhelming; in 1885 the Peabodys moved back to New England, and a year later Mr. Peabody turned to photography full time.

The late nineteenth century, just before the advent of the automobile, was the heyday of rail travel in this country, and Henry Peabody found ready employment at the Boston & Maine Railroad, which hired him to take photographs for the lavishly illustrated travel brochures and souvenir books the railroad used to promote its excursion trains. Mr. Peabody also did landscape, architectural, and marine photography on his own, and quickly became known for his well-composed and evocative photographs of New England. He took first prize in a marine photography exhibition in Boston in 1889, and during the next few years he published two books of photographs, *Representative American Yachts* and *The Coast of Maine.*

By the middle of the 1890s, Henry Peabody was an official photographer for railroads throughout the country during the summer months, traveling wherever the iron rails would take him in search of sweeping vistas, pastoral idylls, and arresting city skylines. He organized his slides and gave lectures about his travels every winter, and also found work as a field photographer in Mexico and Europe.

His wife died in 1898, leaving their eleven-year-old daughter, Mildred Dora, in Mr. Peabody's care. He and his daughter moved to Pasadena, California, in 1902, and he continued to divide his time between the two coasts as a photographer for the Detroit Publishing Company, producer of postcards and travel books. (Many of the photographs of New England shown in this chapter were taken between 1900 and 1908 for the Detroit firm.) As the decades moved on, he polished his travel lectures and took advantage of improved technology that enabled him to make disc recordings of his travelogues synchronized with his photographs and films.

Most of Henry Peabody's New England photographs are representative rather than specific, and the people in them are often anonymous. His work gives the impression that he was interested mainly in places, not people; human beings often seem included as foils to contribute a sense of scale, to emphasize by their diminutiveness the breadth and magnificence of nature or the massive solidity of urban scenes. Yet, if his photographs seem impersonal in a human sense, they establish an intimacy with the setting that preserves for us the historical landscape of New England.

Mr. Peabody died at his home in Glendora, California, in March of 1951 at age ninety-six, a veritable Lowell Thomas of the camera.

A carriage approached the photographer on a
mountain road in the Berkshires of western Massachusetts, just after the turn of the century.

A solitary canoeist paused before the Old North Bridge (of "the shot heard 'round the world" fame) in Concord, Massachusetts, about 1900.

Henry Peabody labeled this tranquil scene "Noon-time." It was taken in Lancaster, Massachusetts, during one of his field trips to New England.

The summit of Mount Tom, near Massachusetts, was a popular picnic spot. A 600-foot
steam-powered tramway brought people up the
mountain to survey the Connecticut River valley.

Woolen bathing suits may have made it easier to stand the chilly water at York Beach, Maine, in 1900.

Shaded by her parasol, a mother watched her children playing on the beach on Pleasure Bay in South Boston. Fort Independence guarded Boston harbor.

Henry Peabody stood on the edge of the Boston
Common, looking toward the Park Street Church, to
record the turn-of-the-century bustle at Park Street
Under, a famous subway stop.

The Swan Boats glided gracefully through the Public Garden, adjacent to the Boston Common, in this view taken about 1906.

The architectural landscape of Boston around the turn of the century included the scenes on these two pages. (Above) The Granary Burying Ground and Park Street Church, looking toward the Common. (Opposite, top) Faneuil Hall, meeting place for Revolutionary firebrands, and today the site of an extensive renovation. (Opposite, bottom) The Public Garden and its equestrian statue of Washington, with Beacon Hill in the background on the left.

16

The age of sail was deferring to the age of steam when this panoramic view of Boston's harbor and waterfront was taken, about 1900.

Fishing schooners tied up near the fish markets at T
Wharf in Boston, about 1904.

Boston's Trinity Church, around 1906, loomed over
a narrow street in an area that today is occupied by
commercial buildings and a parking garage. The old
Hotel Brunswick is on the right.

New Hampshire sailors aboard the U.S.S. *Wabash* formed a musical group that Henry Moore dubbed the Wabash Minstrels. The photograph was taken on the deck of the *Wabash* in a South Carolina port (c. 1863).

Henry P. Moore

During the Civil War, hundreds, perhaps thousands, of amateur and professional photographers used battlefields and encampments as the backdrops to their photographs, lugging their cumbersome equipment through the dusty fields at Gettysburg and across the corpse-strewn meadows at Antietam. Mathew Brady, Alexander Gardner, and others come immediately to mind when we think of the famous stark photographs that documented the struggle, but Henry P. Moore of Concord, New Hampshire, although little known today, was recognized by his contemporaries as a photographer of skill and craftsmanship.

Only the sketchiest biographical details about Mr. Moore have been found. The *Concord City Directory* for 1856 describes him as a boarder with Widow Eliza Moore; for the years 1860, 1864, 1867-68, 1870, and 1872, he is listed as an artist. In 1868 he invented the Silvertype process, used in copying photographs, but it wasn't until 1874, nearly a decade after the Civil War, that he listed himself in the directory as a photographer and advertised a photography-copying business, which continued through the 1880s. Then his career took a rather abrupt turn, for in the 1890s Henry Moore is described as a farmer, poultry breeder, and taxidermist. He went back to artistic pursuits in 1898 as a "painter on china" and in 1900 as a "photographer on china," and then the entries end.

No personal letters, birth or death records, diaries, family photographs, or other private or public documents have been located to use in fleshing out his life. Therefore we don't know why Henry P. Moore went to South Carolina in the winter of 1862 to photograph the Third New Hampshire Regiment as it camped near Hilton Head.

Perhaps he felt like Mathew Brady, who allegedly said, when asked why he decided to photograph the Civil War, "I felt that I had to go. A spirit in my feet said 'go' and I went." Perhaps Henry Moore hoped to make a lot of photographs to copy for the folks back in New Hampshire. He is mentioned in a regimental history of the Third: "Mr. Moore, a photographer from Concord, N.H., began taking pictures the 28th [of February, 1862] in our regiment, principally in groups."

The regiment at that time had not yet engaged in combat, which may account for the casual poses of soldiers lounging outside their tents, reading letters from home, or even enjoying a visit from a spouse. Mr. Moore created an air of optimism, comfort, safety, and everyday normality that helped balance the incongruity of New Hampshire farm boys sweltering in the malaria-ridden Carolina lowlands waiting for the war to reach them. And it did reach many of them: of the 1,534 original volunteers and recruits, 194 died in combat, 148 succumbed to disease, and 487 were wounded and survived, bringing the overall casualty rate to 54 percent. (The Third was one of only three of the eighteen New Hampshire regiments that had more deaths from gunshot wounds than from disease.)

Henry Moore produced reassuringly human, almost domestic, photographs of men who must have been in turn anxious and bored, homesick and restless. At some point — probably by the end of 1863 — he returned to New Hampshire, presumably to sell his photographs. Others of his photographic subjects may survive, but they have not been identified, and Henry Moore and his work fade into obscurity. We can only echo the opinion of *The Philadelphia Photographer,* which in 1865 commented on some of Henry Moore's Civil War photographs: "Aside from this photographic merit which in most cases is considerable, the historical interest they possess is great. . . . Mr. Moore deserves great credit for his enterprise under the difficulties he must have encountered in making these views."

Officers and men of the U.S.S. *Vermont,* moored in Port Royal, South Carolina, posed proudly on deck (c. 1863). Moore's careful composition used the strong lines of the planking and the rigging to integrate the ship with the men.

Military confidence and determination radiate from the officers and crew of the U.S. schooner *C. P. Williams,* photographed in Port Royal, South Carolina (c. 1863). The massive mortar beside the officer was called "Old Abe" by the Union soldiers.

Henry Moore's photographs of the Third New Hampshire Regiment in camp near Hilton Head, South Carolina, placed the New Englanders squarely in their southern setting, often giving the impression they were merely off for a weekend of camping rather than fighting a war. The cook's galley for Company H (above) was capable of turning out three rudimentary meals a day. The quarters of Lieutenants Libby and Hynes (opposite, top) included a clock and other amenities. Surgeon Moulton's wife and son traveled from New Hampshire to join him in camp (opposite, bottom).

Heavy on brass and percussion, the Third New Hampshire's Regimental Band helped relieve the monotony of camp life.

The Third New Hampshire was in camp many months before any combat took place, yet the regimental cemetery inexorably filled with New Hampshire boys who succumbed to disease far from home.

Emma Lewis Coleman, in an undated portrait
(probably early 1890s) found in her portfolio of family photographs.

Emma Lewis Coleman

Born in Boston in 1853 to wealthy parents, Emma Lewis Coleman lived a life dominated by artistic and literary pursuits, punctuated by travel, and enriched by her friendship with artist Susan Minot Lane and historian and teacher C. Alice Baker. Twenty years her senior, these two women had a profound influence on Miss Coleman's own development as a photographer. The three women vacationed together in Deerfield, Massachusetts; York, Maine; the White Mountains of New Hampshire; Quebec; and the Azores. They taught classes together in 1882 for the daughters of former German consul Barthold Schlesinger at his estate, Southwood, in Brookline, Massachusetts, and it is here where Miss Coleman may have learned photography, although she left no record of her first lessons.

Emma Coleman's photographs, taken mainly during the 1880s and 1890s, seem to be strongly influenced by the French Barbizon painters, such as Millet and Corot, whose lush landscapes and idealized views of farmers and rural life provided a nostalgic counterpoint to an increasingly mechanized and urbanized society. Susan Lane, who studied painting under William Morris Hunt, America's leading proponent of the Barbizon school, passed on her insights to Miss Coleman, who later wrote: "Whatever success I have had [as a photographer] is largely due to Miss Lane, of Mr. Hunt's class. She taught me to see a picture."

To Emma Coleman, "seeing" a picture and recording it photographically seem to have been primarily motivated by esthetic considerations rather than historical or personal ones. The people in her photographs were carefully chosen to be picturesque and representative of the mood she wanted to portray, and, like Chansonetta Stanley Emmons but for slightly different reasons, she often photographed several different poses, shifting her models to get just the right effect. She sometimes used local people if they had the proper air of authenticity for her photograph, but she also composed many scenes that featured her friends as "types." The woman washing clothes (page 35) most likely did *not* have her arms in suds every day, but the result was a beautiful and unforgettable photograph; similarly, C. Alice Baker (page 37), dressed in "appropriate" peasant clothing, dragged a calf in front of Emma Coleman's camera for artistic rather than agricultural purposes.

Despite the seriousness with which Emma Coleman approached photography, there is little evidence that she tried to promote her work and gain recognition for her contribution to photography as an art. In the 1890s she began turning to literary and antiquarian pursuits, helping Miss Baker restore Deerfield's Frary House. After Miss Baker's death in 1909, she began to assemble unpublished material that the women had gathered in Canada in the 1880s about New Englanders who had been captured and taken to Canada during the French and Indian Wars. In 1925 she gave more than 250 of her glass negatives to the Society for the Preservation of New England Antiquities, remarking that "it was like giving up part of my life to give them away." In 1942, at age eighty-nine, she died at her home at 42 The Fenway in Boston.

George Sheldon, patriarchal historian of Deerfield, Massachusetts, gazed at an enormous elm that had fallen across the main street in front of his house. The photograph was taken after 1886.

A gypsy couple, on foot from New York, paused
with hurdy-gurdy and tambourine in Deerfield.

The textures of shingles and lush foliage framed a
Northfield Farms, Massachusetts, woman as she
blew a horn to announce the dinner hour, sometime
in the 1880s.

An unnamed model posed in the home of C. Alice
Baker's mother in Cambridge, Massachusetts, in the
mid 1880s, to help create a photograph that used
light and careful composition to transcend its everyday subject matter.

Included in Emma Coleman's studies of country life were these three photographs. A Mr. Gerrish (above) of York, Maine, slowly winnowed beans onto a blanket. The photograph was made between 1883 and 1886. Charcoal burners (opposite, top) lit the kiln at the foot of Mount Agamenticus in York in August of 1884. C. Alice Baker (opposite, bottom), dressed in a country costume, pulled a recalcitrant calf in Deerfield, Massachusetts.

George Henry Donnell, one of Emma Coleman's favorite models in York, maneuvered a skiff full of lobster traps up to the shore.

An unidentified model, possibly the same woman washing clothes (page 35), punted across Chase's Pond in York, in the mid 1880s.

Children played in a yard in Deerfield, mid 1880s.

Hand in hand, two little girls stood beneath the spreading elms that stretched along The Street (what local people called the main street) in Deerfield, Massachusetts, around 1885.

Baldwin Coolidge, in a portrait made before 1917
by John Garo of Boston, whom Coolidge considered
the foremost portrait photographer of his day.

Baldwin Coolidge

There used to be a Baldwin Coolidge Room in the library of the Society for the Preservation of New England Antiquities (SPNEA) presided over by the dignified visage of Mr. Coolidge himself (opposite), a professional photographer whose donation of more than 2,000 glass negatives to the Society in 1918 doubled its photographic collections. The photographs, representing about one tenth of Mr. Coolidge's lifetime work, include hundreds of views of streets and buildings in Boston and nearby towns, scenes from Martha's Vineyard, Nantucket, Woods Hole, and Cape Cod, and pastoral and marine views taken in Windham, New Hampshire, and Biddeford Pool, Maine. Most of the urban photographs were done on assignment or commission; many of those on Cape Cod and the islands may have been inspired more by personal choice, since Mr. Coolidge had a summer home at Cottage City on the Cape. With rare exceptions, the photographs share a straightforward, documentary feeling, their details captured by an unsparingly sharp focus that shunned more impressionistic methods. Technically adroit and unfailingly well-composed, the Coolidge photographs also include some, like the ones on pages 44 and 55, of great delicacy and suggestiveness.

Baldwin Coolidge, whose extensive work can only be hinted at by this chapter, was born in July of 1845 in Woburn, Massachusetts, to a distinguished New England family that traced its descent back to the *Mayflower's* Elder Brewster. Coolidge was named for his great-great-grandfather, Loammi Baldwin, whose 1661 mansion adjoined the Coolidge farm. Mr. Coolidge served in the Civil War in Company K of the Sixth Massachusetts Regiment of the Light Artillery; soon after his discharge he married Lucy Ann Plumer, and became the first city engineer of Lawrence, Massachusetts. In 1878 he turned from engineering to photography and opened a studio on Tremont Street in Boston. He also taught clay modeling, and was hired as the staff photographer for the Museum of Fine Arts.

Coolidge apparently received many commissions from Bostonians for portraits and architectural photographs, and he insisted, unlike most professionals, on doing most of his own processing and printing. William Sumner Appleton, founder of the SPNEA and one of the first archivists to avidly collect photographs as a documentary source, recalled going to Coolidge's studio both as a boy and as a young man to buy prints.

In 1908, four years after his wife's death, Baldwin Coolidge moved his studio to 410A Boylston Street, where he continued to work until failing health forced his retirement. He left the family farm in Woburn in 1917, at age seventy-two, to live with his only child, Marie (Mrs. J. H. Henry), in what he referred to as "the loneliness and homesickness of this sunshiny and flowery land of murders, divorces and burglars" — Pasadena, California. His longtime assistant, Mrs. Marie Howe, doggedly tried to help caption and date the 2,000 photographs donated to the SPNEA; but since Mr. Coolidge had always adamantly refused to classify his photographs by subject and cross-reference them, many captions are sketchy at best. Baldwin Coolidge died in California in 1928 at age eighty-three.

Spectators on high ground surveyed the floodwaters
that poured through Linden Park in the Roxbury
section of Boston in 1886.

The flood turned Vernon Street in Roxbury into a canal; Mr. Coolidge and his tripod may have stood in a foot of water to take this photograph.

The worst of the 1886 flooding had begun to subside
in Roxbury when this photograph was made.

A carriage waited at the foot of Mount Vernon
Street on Beacon Hill in Boston, in the 1890s.

This unusually sentimental (for Baldwin Coolidge)
pastoral scene was photographed at Kendall's Mill-
pond in Windham, New Hampshire, June 15, 1891.

A more typically straightforward rural view depicted the Shield family in front of their Windham, New Hampshire, homestead.

Fishermen in Biddeford Pool, Maine, split cod to prepare them for drying and salting. This scene was photographed October 8, 1907.

George W. Winslow of Nantucket displayed the jaw-bone of a shark in a photograph taken in the 1890s.

A visitor to Martha's Vineyard looked out over the
lagoon at Cottage City sometime in the 1890s (top);
fishing and pleasure boats ringed the harbor at Sias-
conset (S'conset) on Nantucket in 1887 (bottom).

"Rusticators" on Martha's Vineyard set out for the
cliffs at Gay Head (top); another holiday group
boarded the excursion boat *Vigilant* at Woods Hole,
near Falmouth, Massachusetts, in 1897 (bottom).

Fishing shacks perched on a peaceful tidal inlet at
Biddeford Pool, Maine, around 1900.

A silent figure observed the wreck of the *Minnie C.* on Nantucket, sometime between 1885 and 1890.

Frederick B. Quimby with his camera, probably about 1890.

Ella York of Wollaston, Massachusetts, demonstrated the patented "Quimby's Focusing Attachment" that eliminated the awkward focusing cloth.

Fred Quimby's studio at Ground Nut Hill in Cape Neddick, Maine (shown in August of 1894), featured his photographs and other local artwork.

Frederick B. Quimby

Frederick Quimby's family — the Rayneses, the Swetts, the Donnells, the Quimbys — had lived in York, Maine, since the 1700s, farming, fishing, digging clams, cutting wood, harvesting potatoes, making cider as the seasons progressed. Fred's father, Ira, moved to Boston to become a carpenter, but he married Lucy Raynes of York in 1854 and kept close ties with the families at home. Fred, their third son, was born in 1862, and made frequent visits to his grandparents' farms on Raynes Neck and Cape Neddick, near York.

It is not known when Fred Quimby began to take photographs, but early on he described himself as an artist and photographer. He may have had a studio at his winter home in Malden, Massachusetts; he certainly had one at Ground Nut Hill, the family homestead in Cape Neddick, which Quimby used as his headquarters from June through October every year. In 1890 he received a patent for "Quimby's Focusing Attachment," a device shaped like a hand mirror with eyepieces attached, which could be used without having to throw the focusing cloth over one's head.

In a sense, Fred Quimby's photographs make a family album, for his subjects are his uncles, aunts, cousins, and other relatives and friends in York. He clearly delighted in making very personal portraits and records of family affairs: the Sunday afternoon chess game, the baby's bath, cousin Elinor Raynes in the Devil's Armchair. But he also used his family in a more public sense as models, for he sold prints of many photographs that he made in Maine. "Springtime on the Farm," "Summer on the Farm," and similar titles were among the copyrighted folios he offered for sale at his studio.

Quimby seems to have intentionally set his subjects into carefully chosen and congenial settings that give each exposure a sense of place and time and permanence. Photographs like the plowing and harvesting scenes that follow abound in his work and give a fascinating documentary look at agricultural activity in the late nineteenth century.

Fred Quimby married Cora Donnell of York in 1895, and their son, Charles Frederick, was born the following year. On December 2, 1896, Fred Quimby died at age 34, probably of tuberculosis, at his Malden home. His wife died in South Carolina the next year, also of tuberculosis, and their little boy was raised by his maternal grandparents in York. Fred Quimby is buried in the parish cemetery in York, Maine, his grave passed unknowingly by the hundreds of thousands of tourists who swarm to the Maine coast every summer in search of a remnant of what Fred Quimby saw there.

Fred Quimby (foreground, squeezing camera bulb release) and a young niece or cousin posed in the doorway of the family homestead at Raynes Neck in York, Maine. The Raynes home had been built in 1700, and the photographer appreciated its beauty as a setting for photographs.

Ralph Quimby, Fred's older brother, was a civil engineer and painter. Two neighbors watched him sketching oxen in Sam Payne's field in York, in the early 1890s.

A cousin, probably Elinor Raynes, reclined in the Devil's Armchair, an unusual rock formation at Seabury, near York. This photograph, with its pleasing repetition of curved line, was made between 1890 and 1893.

A leisurely chess game took up a sunny afternoon at one of the family farms near York, Maine. Quimby is at the right, with the telltale camera cable.

Fred Quimby photographed himself with Ella York and a young boy, probably in Malden, Massachusetts, about 1890. Ella York's connection with Quimby is not clear. She may have been a model who worked in his Malden studio, yet this photograph suggests a closer relationship.

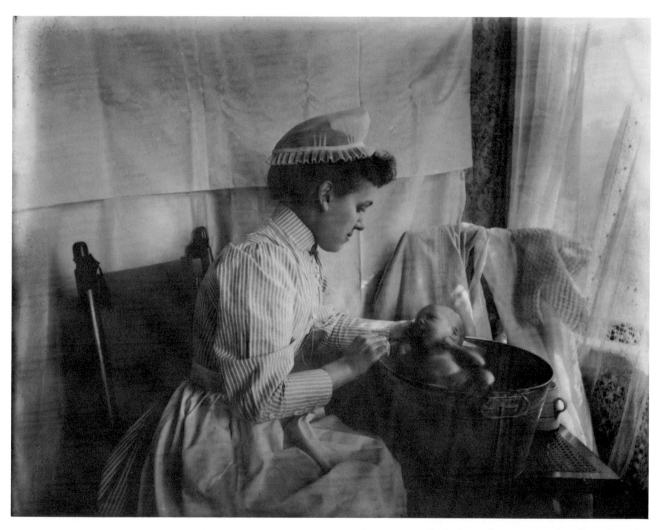

Aunt Lucy Quimby, whose attire implies that she was a nurse, bathed a small baby. If the soft focus and intimacy of this photograph are any clue, the baby may possibly have been Fred and Cora Quimby's son, Charles Frederick Quimby.

Little John Hill, peeking out from under his hat brim, helped Shaw Raynes pick up apples in the orchard at the Raynes farm in October of 1890.

Quimby called this photograph "Carman's pet lamb." It was taken in York, probably late one fall.

"Springtime on the Farm," one of Quimby's portfo-
lios of rural life, may have included this early spring
plowing scene in York.

Fall of 1892 found Mr. Earle and his son William harvesting potatoes at Fred Quimby's farm, Ground Nut Hill, in Cape Neddick.

Fred Quimby photographed the Swett homestead
in Cape Neddick at every season of the year. This
summer scene included Aunt May at the gate, Aunt
Lucy under the tree, and Aunt Lizzie near the road.

Although many of Fred Quimby's country photographs seem primarily intended to document farm activities, he also saw the more idyllic side of rural life, as this romantic view down Wood Road on Raynes Neck suggests. The photograph was taken in October of 1895, only a year before the photographer's untimely death.

Lena Osgood (later Long) was photographed in her
flower garden in East Pittsford about 1905.

Lena Osgood Long

One warm day in July of 1975, Lorraine Moore of the Saxtons River (Vermont) Historical Society got a telephone call from Doris Osgood Camp. Doris and her husband, Elisha, were preparing to sell at auction the furnishings of a house on Pleasant Street in Saxtons River that they had inherited from Doris's aunt, Lena Osgood Long. Did Mrs. Moore want to take a look at a bunch of pictures in old paper bags in the attic? Lorraine Moore remembered Mrs. Long, who had died in 1967, as a prim little lady who had rarely ventured out of her house except to attend church or to work in her flower gardens.

The tattered bags held 353 mounted photographs that had been taken by Lena Osgood Long during a period in her life that most townspeople had forgotten about or never known. A wooden crate holding 228 glass plates, each in its original envelope and with its exposure noted in Lena's meticulous handwriting, revealed that for about fifteen years, from roughly 1892 until 1908, she had been a serious photographer — serious enough, at least, to lug her heavy camera and glass plates around the landscape, to keep in a notebook a record of subjects and exposure data, and to print and mount her own pictures. Her rosewood Korona VII camera (manufactured by the Gundlach Optical Company of Rochester, New York, before 1894), well-preserved and fitted with a Rapid Rectigraphic 5 x 7 lens, also came to light and was donated along with the photographs to the historical society.

Lena Osgood Long's biography has many gaps. Local historians in Saxtons River learned that she was born July 15, 1871, in East Pittsford, Vermont, a small hill town just north of Rutland. She attended Castleton Normal School and taught in West Rutland at a one-room school with forty pupils who were "inclined to be noisy," she reported in a diary. While she was in West Rutland, Lena Osgood attended the Baptist Church four times a week, went ice-skating, traveled by train to the World's Columbian Exposition in Chicago in August of 1893, and at some point started taking photographs.

She lived at her parents' farmhouse in East Pittsford, and from there set out on foot or by carriage to visit friends and record favorite scenes and events. She clambered around the pilings of the Chittenden and East Pittsford dams, under construction between 1900 and 1905, to photograph workers and surveyors, making eighty-three prints in all. She also photographed landscapes and flowers, but some of her most appealing photographs are the informal portraits she made of friends and neighbors in East Pittsford. One of her favorite subjects was Harley Perkins (a neighbor, certainly a friend, and perhaps a former beau) and his family as they worked on their farm. Most of her photographs are straightforward, well-composed scenes of rural life, warmed by her concentration on friends and relatives.

Lena Osgood married Arthur Long, a friend of some years, on December 30, 1908. Mr. Long did YMCA work in various parts of the country, and he and Lena lived in Cleveland, Denver, and Rensselaer (near Albany) after their marriage. In 1926 they moved to Saxtons River, where Lena's brother lived, bringing Lena's aged mother to live with them. After her marriage Lena Osgood Long evidently stopped taking photographs. She never mentioned photography in her diary, and no photographs later than 1908 have been located.

The Longs had no children. Mrs. Long was often seen working in her flower gardens, and was said to have a ready smile for the neighbors' children. She started a Sunday school class for women, and with her husband read the entire Bible thirteen times a year. As she got older she kept more and more to herself, and became known as a rather eccentric woman who kept her floors and furniture covered with newspapers. After Arthur Long's death in 1956, Lena Osgood Long lived alone in the big house on Pleasant Street until her own death in 1967 at age ninety-six. Perhaps she occasionally climbed slowly to the attic to sift through her photographs of another time, another place.

Lena Osgood photographed Harley Perkins and his family, along with Arthur Long (right), at the Perkins' farmhouse, probably around 1908.

No documentary of Vermont farm life could exclude the cow. This was Uncle Nathan Davis of East Pittsford with a beautiful Holstein, about 1900.

(Above) Haying was a family affair: this scene was photographed at the Perkins' farm in East Pittsford, with Harley astride the new mowing machine, and his wife, Rosie, and sons handling the rakes. (Opposite, top) Harley Perkins' two-horsepower sawmill used a treadmill system to run a drag saw. Harley's Morgans and his ox team got into the picture along with Harley (left) and sons Harris and Hugh (on stump). (Opposite, bottom) An unidentified hunting party, photographed with Lena Osgood's usual straight-on clarity, posed with its quarry.

(Opposite, top) A Mr. Libbey (left) joined Harley Perkins, his son Hugh, and Harley's Morgan horse before Lena Osgood's camera one winter day about 1903. (Opposite, bottom) Cutting firewood meant long hours with a sawhorse and bucksaw. The Osgoods' hired man, Mr. Matthews, paused to be photographed about 1900. (Above) Warmed by fur robes, a woman and child set off by sleigh from the East Pittsford home of Willard Osgood (the photographer's father) around the turn of the century.

Harley Perkins (left) used his ox team to gather
maple sap during the snowless spring of 1907.

"Sugaring off," with its feast of maple syrup poured over snow, was an annual occasion at Charles Pike's sugarhouse in East Pittsford.

(Opposite, top) Lena Osgood taught in a one-room school similar to this one. She labeled this photograph "Edith's schoolhouse." (Opposite, bottom) A placid stream made wading irresistible to this group of youngsters. (Above) Two children enjoyed a wagon ride, probably in East Pittsford.

George Tingley made this self-portrait in his studio
in Mystic in 1899.

"The Light Beyond"

George Edward Tingley

George Tingley, born in Mystic, Connecticut, in 1864, spent his entire long and productive life in that prosperous fishing village at the mouth of the Mystic River on Long Island Sound. When he was a young man, of an age to choose a profession, his father became quite anxious about George's future and suggested many possibilities: boat builder, locomotive engineer, machinist. George hesitated. Then one day his father came home with the news that the local photographer, E. A. Schofield, was looking for an apprentice. As George recalled years later in his memoirs, "Tho' I had been unable to name the line of life work that would be most suitable and satisfying to me, his probings had finally hit the nail so squarely on the head as to cause me to exclaim, 'Eureka! Selah!'" His apprenticeship began on January 1, 1884. Within ten years he bought out Schofield and began to make a name for himself as a portrait and landscape photographer, or "photographist," as he put it.

Tingley was a familiar sight in Mystic. He played cornet in the town brass band, was a charter member of the Mystic Hook and Ladder Company, and served as tax collector. On weekends, when he wasn't in his studio making formal portraits, he was out tramping in the fields and along the Mystic River, his heavy camera and tripod over his shoulder, looking for appealing scenes. (He was always on foot: he never owned a horse or a car, and it's said that the only time he ever rented a buggy was on his wedding day.) He seemed never to run out of subjects; he seemed never to yearn for exotic settings. Tingley looked at life in his small community and found a fascinating cast of characters, timeless pastoral landscapes, the dignity of daily life. He had a natural gift for composition, and he developed special printing techniques by studying the photographic periodicals of the day, but he had no other formal training in art or photography.

Especially during the two decades before World War I, George Tingley's photographs were known and appreciated in the United States and Europe. Eastman Kodak published a selection of his photographs in the December 1916 issue of *Studio Light*, the magazine for professional photographers, and several of Tingley's photographs won prestigious international awards. To a modern eye, some of his photographs appear to be infused with Victorian sentimentality, obvious symbolism, and the murky "Rembrandt lighting" so popular around the turn of the century. Yet even his posed studio portraits show an unfailing instinct for detail and effective lighting, and many of his landscapes have an abstract quality that appeals to the most modern connoisseur.

"The Light Beyond" (left) was Tingley's most famous picture. It was used on the cover of the British publication *Photograms* in 1899 with this comment: " . . . It has the charm of the best of the 'moaning eventide' work, plus a note of optimism or faith; and may fairly be described as one of the pictures of which very few are produced in any one year — a picture that will live." The photograph also won a silver medal at the International Exhibition in Moscow, and it was reported in the Mystic newspaper that the Duchess of Sermonita, lady-in-waiting to the Queen of Italy, had requested a print.

When George Tingley was seventy-five, a fire in his studio destroyed most of his equipment and a good portion of his life's work. The glass plates and prints that survived were his personal favorites, taken mostly between 1895 and 1916, and stored at home. After his studio burned, Tingley retired and began writing his memoirs. He took no more photographs. During the day he often walked to the firehouse to talk with his friends. Tingley was ninety-four when he died in 1958.

A courting couple strolled along River Road in Mystic, Connecticut, a romantic scene replaced today by a multi-lane interstate highway overpass.

Since family tradition has it that George Tingley rented a buggy only on his wedding day, he either walked or was a passenger in a friend's carriage the day he photographed this bucolic scene near Mystic.

"A very dear friend," wrote George Tingley in his memoirs, "who many times had conveyed me and my impediments to more distant fields in search of new scenes, remarked that it was almost impossible to get me past any field in which was to be seen cattle, sheep, or an occasional horse. . . . My friend, an enthusiastic amateur, wishing to accompany me on some of my rambles, joined me on one of my Sabbath walks. . . . A flock of sheep attracted my attention because it represented all branches of the sheep family, including many ewes, some young lambs, and one large ram." On this occasion, George Tingley was charged by the ram, much to the amusement of his friend, who remained in safety on the other side of a stone wall. The photographs on these two pages demonstrate Tingley's affection for domestic animals as photographic subjects.

(Opposite, top) George Tingley didn't have to walk far out of town to find scenes of pastoral beauty along the river. Another artist (far left in photo) also recorded the beauty of the scene. (Opposite, bottom) Tingley called this photograph "The Old Settler," and probably asked Bill Jackson to walk slowly past his house one day when the light was just right. (Above) Two farmers used a flatboat to haul a load of salt marsh hay upstream, past the present site of the Mystic Seaport Museum. The hay was commonly harvested for use as fertilizer.

The subject of this winsome portrait is unknown, but she may have been a little girl Tingley described in his memoirs. He once visited a local family and offered candy to an appealing five-year-old, who helped herself to a piece. Her mother, Tingley reported, prompted her: "Hope, what do you say to the gentleman?" The little girl, lifting her eyes shyly to Tingley, lisped, "Thave the reth 'til morning?"

This lovely subject was Harriet Cheney, who taught at the grammar school in Mystic Bridge. She later married Laurence Griswold of Batavia, New York, publisher of *The Daily News* in that town, and had two children. This portrait was probably made sometime after 1910.

One Captain Crouch, photographed in George
Tingley's studio, was a Quaker, locally famous for
his outspoken pacifism.

Mrs. Nancy Chapman posed for George Tingley in his studio at his request, and the result was this photograph that won a prize in a contest in France. She is holding an original Nantucket basket.

Henry Hadcock was fond of making informal portraits of his neighbors. This group under an apple tree was probably the Jack Lawson family at 3 Oakland Street in Roxbury, Massachusetts. (No portrait of Hadcock himself has been located.)

Henry L. Hadcock

Henry L. Hadcock, born in upstate New York in 1856, came to Boston as a boy of sixteen. He took a room in a boardinghouse and soon found a job in a drugstore as a clerk, determined to work his way up to owning his own pharmacy. By 1876, when he was twenty, the hard-working young man with an aptitude for chemistry and business had acquired his own apothecary shop at 2700 Washington Street in Roxbury, which at the time boasted of being the geographical center of Boston.

Hadcock boarded at nearby rooming houses until 1880, when the *Boston City Directory* shows that he owned a house at 2702 Washington Street, either beside or above his pharmacy. He was to hone his skills as a pharmacist for fifty-five years, making Hadcock's Apothecary a landmark in Roxbury. His life was consolidated into a compact sphere with the store and his home as the center. He married, had a daughter and a son, and lived in the house on Washington Street up to his death.

Henry Hadcock probably began taking photographs when he was in his thirties. It appears that he was elected to the Boston Society of Amateur Photographers during the 1880s (reorganized as the Boston Camera Club in 1886), for his signature is on a members' list in a book about the club's meetings. An enthusiastic amateur, he applied a pharmacist's precision and attention to detail to his new hobby, creating photographs of wonderful clarity and refinement. He concentrated on his neighborhood, taking carefully balanced photographs of the grocery next door, the furniture store down the street, and his neighbors in their backyards.

In the early 1890s Hadcock took a series of photographs at Wheaton College, a school for women, in Norton, Massachusetts. He photographed dormitory rooms, public drawing rooms, genteel games of lawn tennis, and neatly composed groups of co-eds strumming banjos and acting giddy and sentimental by turns. A note on the back of one of the photographs relates that some of them were published in 1893 in a book of views of the school.

Few of Henry Hadcock's surviving photographs were taken after the turn of the century, and it is unclear whether he continued to enjoy his hobby. In December 1931 Mr. Hadcock died at age seventy-seven. His obituary in the *Boston Evening Transcript* did not mention his interest in photography.

Henry Hadcock's drugstore at Dale and Washington
Streets in Roxbury was stocked with neat rows of
chemicals and medicines, cigars and sponges, and
even a pay telephone.

Grocery delivery wagons were ready to roll at Robert McCullagh's grocery at 2706-2708 Washington Street in Roxbury, adjoining Hadcock's Apothecary.

The New Roxbury Market, known in the neighborhood as Casey's Market, filled its windows with meat, fruit, and seafood fresh from Boston's Fish Pier.

According to Henry Hadcock's notation on this photograph, Casey of Casey's Market (opposite) also owned the carpet and furniture store (above) just down the street in Roxbury.

The Greenwood family, probably neighbors of Henry Hadcock, brought out bicycles and chairs for an informal summer portrait complete with hammock and Japanese lanterns.

A child's playroom at the Jack Lawson home in Roxbury was a Victorian dream of china dolls, wicker carriages, and knickknacks to spare. Judging from the blackboard, this was baby Chester's room in 1890.

Possibly working on assignment, Henry Hadcock made a series of photographs at Wheaton College, a girls' school in Norton, Massachusetts. The date was the early 1890s, a time (at least for daughters of the well-to-do) of frills and furbelows, sentiment and sentimentality, bonneted skulls on headboards (opposite, bottom), songs strummed on banjos, and sedate sessions of lawn tennis.

John Conness promenaded with his family on the
curving drive of their estate on River Street in the
Mattapan section of Dorchester, along the Neponset
River. Although the Boston suburbs were beginning
to engulf large estates like this one, Conness ran the
property as a farm, and considered himself a gentleman farmer.

Conness, an Irishman who had been a Senator from California before moving to Dorchester after the Civil War, had this view from his study. Conness, the last surviving pallbearer from Abraham Lincoln's funeral, died in 1909.

Warwick Stevens Carpenter, with an unidentified
companion, in a self-portrait at his camp in Woodford, Vermont, about 1900.

Warwick Stevens Carpenter

When Warwick Stevens Carpenter died in Santa Barbara, California, in 1966 at age eighty-five, he was well known as a business economist and market analyst who had a special interest in promoting travel and tourism. Before moving to California in 1923, he had been the secretary of the New York Conservation Commission, editor of *The Journal of the Outdoor Life* and *The Conservationist,* and a member of the Explorers Club. He had published several wilderness-travel books and wildlife studies, as well as a book on winter camping (1913) and one called *The Summer Paradise in History* (1914), a glowing collection of facts and lore about Lake Champlain and the Adirondacks.

But of his earlier life, especially before and during the time that the following photographs were taken, only a few facts are known. Warwick Stevens Carpenter was born in Hoosick Falls, New York (about five miles from the Vermont border), on April 7, 1881. He graduated from Columbia University in 1904 and married Jean Simmons on August 1, 1905. The couple lived in Bennington, Vermont, for some time before moving to New York State. They had a son, who was named for his father. From then on, the biographical details focus on professional accomplishments, except to note that his wife died in 1949 after a long illness. Nowhere in public records about his life is his photography mentioned.

Carpenter's love for the outdoors and for the recreational attractions of the Lake Champlain area — his "summer paradise" — is apparent in his photographs, which were found in the late 1970s when ownership of a camp in Woodford, Vermont, that had long been in Carpenter's family, changed hands. Glass negatives were discovered in the loft of the log cabin that had been a favorite haven for Mr. Carpenter during his youth and college years, the time when these photographs were made.

It is not known how often Mr. Carpenter and his family returned to the camp in Woodford, nor even whether he continued to take photographs. Perhaps the carefree days of snowshoeing in the woods and swimming in Lake Champlain seemed like a golden time that could be savored, but never repeated.

Motorists crossed a narrow bridge, possibly near
Hoosick Falls, New York, near the Vermont border
(top); a carriage appeared to make better time on a
country lane (bottom).

The excursion steamer *Vermont* made regular trips down Lake Champlain around the turn of the century (top); passengers disembarked from a smaller steamboat near the foot of the lake (bottom).

Dressed in a typical 1900 bathing costume of wool-
en dress and stockings, a pert swimmer combed the
snarls out of her hair.

Another decorously dressed bather enjoyed aiming
her new Kodak box camera at friends in the water,
possibly Lake Champlain.

Mixed doubles in both tennis (background) and
lawn bowling were enjoyed at this resort, probably
in the Adirondacks during Warwick Stevens Carpenter's college years.

An artist caught a good likeness of his subject; the photograph may have been made at the Carpenters' home in Bennington, Vermont, after 1905.

Mr. Carpenter and his friends clearly enjoyed the outdoor life, and he often entertained groups of young people. The camp scenes on these pages were taken in the early 1900s, either near the Carpenter camp in Woodford, Vermont, or in the Adirondacks, his two favorite haunts.

Frederick W. Greene, in his Andover, Massachusetts, study in 1892 (possibly a self-portrait).

Frederick W. Greene

Frederick W. Greene, born in Brattleboro, Vermont, in 1859, was a Congregational minister and devoted father and husband who made more than 1,500 photographs on glass negatives between 1890 and 1914. Most of the photographs by this talented amateur are pleasing, idyllic scenes of family and friends in successful pursuit of happiness in New England — a charmed world in peaceful repose. Naturally the confidant of many because of his role as a minister, Frederick Greene also had a special rapport with children (he had six of his own) that gave him numerous willing and photogenic models.

Much of the Greene family's life revolved around a rambling two-story house called the Manse in Jaffrey Center, New Hampshire. The house, which had a sweeping view of Mount Monadnock and was the summer destination of the family each year, was built in 1788 by Mr. Greene's great-grandfather, the Reverend Laban Ainsworth, who was Jaffrey's first minister (for seventy-six years) and who lived to be 101 years old.

While Frederick Greene was a student at Amherst College, he often brought his friends from the Class of 1882 to Jaffrey to spend the summers with him, and after graduation four college mates, also Congregational ministers, built summer homes nearby in the shadow of the broad-shouldered mountain. Mr. Greene loved to organize overnight camping trips, often including as many as twenty people, to see the sunrise from the top of Monadnock. He institutionalized an annual Fourth of July picnic at Thorndike Pond for the families of all those '82 classmates, a tradition that family members still observe. He also helped his children make exotic costumes out of old clothing in the attic, and photographed the pageants they put on.

Each year when September arrived, the Greenes reluctantly headed home to the parsonages in Andover, Massachusetts, and later in Middletown, Connecticut, where Mr. Greene's parishes were located. He seems to have taken fewer photographs at home than he did at the Manse, but would bring out his camera for special occasions and holidays, especially Christmas. He developed his own negatives and made prints, many of which can be found today in the fading family albums.

Whether he was photographing a hay cart composed against mountain and sky or a picnic on the grass, Greene seems to have pictured nature as a peaceable kingdom — a world removed from tragedy or strife. He may have absorbed this viewpoint from Benjamin Champney, a landscape painter and family friend, six of whose paintings hung in the Manse. Or, he may have sensed that his own life was special — that he had been spared many of the perils of living in a rapidly changing world. If Greene sought to commemorate his moments of tranquility in his pictures, then he succeeded admirably at the task.

Upon his death at age sixty-one in 1920, Frederick Greene was buried in the family plot near the Jaffrey Center Meetinghouse. His glass negatives, stored in lightproof boxes by a thoughtful relative, nested in the attic of the Manse until the family decided to reprint them in 1981. Among his other effects was an 1887 edition of *Wilson's Quarter Century in Photography,* with this inscription: "The camera is mightier than the pen or the pencil."

Jaffrey Center, New Hampshire, summer residents paused at the Halfway House on Mount Monadnock (bottom), then finished ascending the 3,165-foot peak to appreciate the view (top).

Greene daughters Anna and Dorothy (top) could see all the way to Boston in 1908 from the heights of the mountain. The Greene, Bliss, and Bixler families posed on Monadnock's rocky summit (bottom).

Frederick Greene (right) and two companions pic-
nicked in the woods near the Thorndike Club in
Jaffrey Center. Greene used a bulb release to take
the photograph.

The Greene children and friends embarked on a voyage around Thorndike Pond in their St. Lawrence rowboat. Frederick Greene was present, as usual, to record their fun.

Summer for the Greene family included a steady
round of hikes, picnics, and amateur theatricals.
The stage (above), possibly in the Jaffrey Center
Meetinghouse, seems set for a Fourth of July perfor-
mance. The parsonage in Andover (opposite, top)
was probably decorated for a Memorial Day tab-
leau, about 1905. The highlight of another summer
was an exotic bazaar (opposite, bottom) by the
meetinghouse carriage sheds.

The Hall children, neighbors of the Greenes in Andover, Massachusetts, gathered on the rose-bedecked porch at the parsonage sometime in the early 1890s.

Charles Phelps drove his ox-drawn hay cart up South Hill Road in Jaffrey Center toward the meetinghouse, with Mount Monadnock beyond. He was a blind man who farmed for decades in town and delivered milk to local people.

In another scene from Frederick Greene's family
album, three Greene children acted as the pony for
two passengers in a little buckboard.

Mr. Greene's concentration on his children resulted in several beautiful informal portraits such as this: son Theodore hugged his little brother Walter, probably on the porch of the Andover home about 1895.

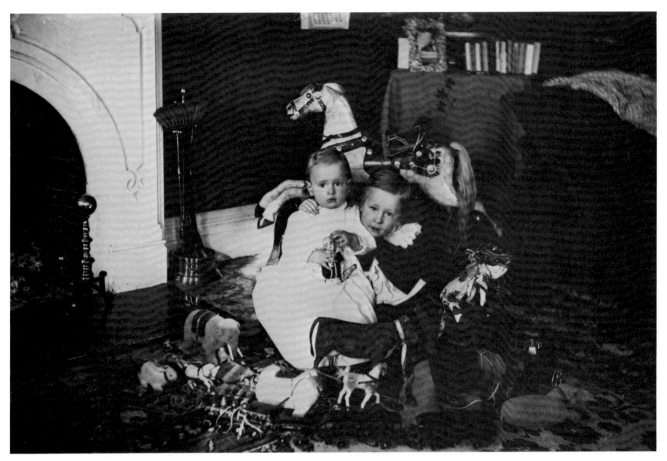

Christmas of 1894 at the Andover parsonage featured a sure-footed rocking horse for Walter and
Theodore, and a garlanded Christmas tree fit for
storybook children.

Wilfred E. Stone, in a portrait made about 1930.

Wilfred E. Stone

Wilfred Eugene Stone was born in Cranston, Rhode Island, on October 22, 1880, the son of Charles and Selinda (Howard) Stone. The young man graduated from Cranston High School in 1898, married Edith A. Platt in 1899, and spent the rest of his long life in the Knightsville section of Cranston. He made his living as a reporter for the *Providence Journal,* writing what newspapers call "human interest" stories and often illustrating them with his own photographs.

Mr. Stone's personal life centered around his family (he and Edith had three daughters and one son) and community affairs. He was a volunteer at the Knightsville Congregational Church from 1909 until 1928, when he became the beloved pastor of the congregation, serving until his death in the spring of 1957. He built the pulpit for the church, and set up a small print shop in the basement (where he produced children's stories as well as church bulletins). Mr. Stone, who even served as Cranston's dog officer for a number of years, also was the unofficial local historian, and long after his retirement from the *Journal* was contributing historical photographs (usually taken by himself) and vignettes to the "Echoes of Cranston" column in the *Cranston Herald.*

In his role as a roving reporter for the *Journal,* Mr. Stone cast a curious and affectionate eye on local affairs, lugging his cumbersome glass-negative camera (and often one or more of his children) around Rhode Island to photograph parades, children, immigrants, holidays, gas station attendants, orphanages, church suppers, kids playing marbles, street fairs, and, in one surviving print, his own kitchen sink. He did photo essays that documented local industries — ice harvesting, cranberry picking, oyster shucking — and caught the complexities of a rapidly changing society after the turn of the century. His natural warmth and neighborly rapport brought an intimacy to his photographs that went beyond photojournalism and revealed the personalities behind local events. While the instinctive historian in Wilfred Stone produced a precise record of Rhode Island life during the early years of this century, the "human interest" photographer in him created a celebration of community life.

Wilfred Stone took photographs up to the time of his death at age seventy-six, when his legacy — four thousand surviving glass negatives — was put into storage. In 1978, his great-granddaughter began the laborious yet exciting task of printing, cataloging, and preserving the photographs it had taken Wilfred Stone a lifetime to make.

The Civil War was sixty years behind them when these veterans, members of the Grand Army of the Republic, saluted young patriots rehearsing for Memorial Day exercises in Cranston in 1925.

Shriners paraded Old Glory through the streets of
Newport in an enthusiastic parade in 1920.

A new Texaco service station on Exchange Place in
Providence was an eye-catching reminder that the
auto age was in full swing in 1920.

An insurance broker was framed in the doorway of his office in South County, Rhode Island, in this haunting portrait made about 1920.

Wilfred Stone photographed this group of Cranston
boys intent on a curbside game of marbles.

Patrons perused the offerings of a street fair, probably in Cranston.

Immigrants debarked in about 1920 from a Portu-
guese schooner berthed at State Pier in Providence,
a common point of entry. Many immigrants found
work in Rhode Island's textile factories in the early
decades of this century.

The oyster-shucking industry employed many Italian immigrants. By 1930, when Wilfred Stone took this photograph, shuckers worked at automatic conveyor belts and rinsing machines.

Harold L. Dewing, busy with his wireless radio in this 1921 photograph, was one of the founding members of the Providence Technical High School Radio Club.

Wilfred Stone's series of photographs on the local cranberry industry included this portrayal of a young picker at Grass Pond Bog in Coventry, 1920. School children and unemployed mill workers could earn two cents a quart for harvesting the crimson berries each fall.

Wilfred Stone visited the Lakeside Home, a health
camp on Warwick Lake established for children suf-
fering from tuberculosis, which was treated then
only with fresh air and sunshine. He photographed
this young mother and her baby in 1921.

Iva Stone, the photographer's daughter, was a favorite subject. This 1910 photograph shows her seated on the back steps of their Cranston home.

Wilfred Stone photographed the kitchen sink in his
house on D Street in Cranston about 1930.

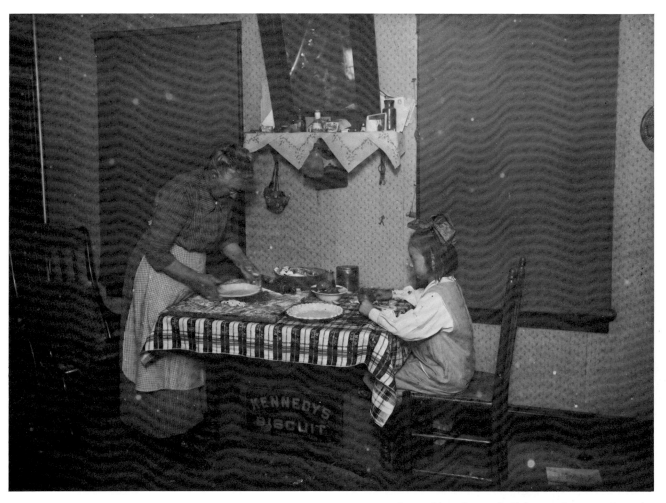

Experienced hands made light work preparing pies for a Thanksgiving feast in 1921.

Before the days of refrigeration, farm families often cut ice from ponds during the winter as a source of extra income. The slabs were floated over to a conveyor belt and loaded into wagons. This scene was on the Knight farm, 1910.

An exuberant troupe of sledders poised on the top
of a hill one exhilarating winter day, about 1920.

Chansonetta Stanley Emmons, in a formal portrait
about 1890.

This photograph of Mrs. Emmons, taken toward the
end of her life, was made atop Mount Mansfield,
Vermont, in the 1930s.

Chansonetta Stanley Emmons

We may feel that we are looking back to the turn of the century when we view Chansonetta Stanley Emmons' photographs of Kingfield and West New Portland, Maine, but more than any other photographer in this book, Mrs. Emmons' intention was to look back even further, to reconstruct the way of life in interior Maine at the time of her own childhood. Born in Kingfield on December 30, 1858, Chansonetta was the only daughter among the seven children of Solomon and Apphia Stanley. Admittedly a spoiled and headstrong girl, she acquired early-on a sense of pride and confidence in her talents as an artist. The year she spent at Western State Normal School (1876-77) in Farmington, Maine, reinforced her desire to become an artist, and from there she went to stay with her brother F. E. in Lewiston, Maine, to study drawing. It was probably at this time that she first became interested in photography. (Her brothers F. E. and F. O. developed the Stanley photographic dry plate, which they eventually sold to Eastman Kodak. They are probably better known for their automobile, the Stanley Steamer.)

Chansonetta went on to study art in Boston and there met and married James Nathaniel Whitman Emmons in 1887. Their daughter Dorothy was born in 1891. Tragedy struck in 1898, when James died suddenly of blood poisoning at the age of forty-one, leaving his wife with little money and a young child. Mrs. Emmons' brother F. O. began paying rent for her at a duplex in Newton, Massachusetts (which he continued to do until her death).

To recover her equilibrium, Mrs. Emmons retreated that winter, along with Dorothy, to the family home in Kingfield and it was then that she began to take the series of photographs for which she is remembered. Always a proper Victorian lady, she kept busy with her painting and photography, which brought in precious little money, and preferred to live on an allowance from her brothers rather than to seek more remunerative work. She spent countless hours visiting friends and relatives in Kingfield and West New Portland, clearly expecting them to pose for her camera for hours at a time to create a photograph that would capture, at least for her, the perfected memory of her Kingfield childhood.

Mrs. Emmons used only natural light for interior shots, and since she never used a light meter, she often had to guess at exposure times. For time exposures she would simply hold the shutter open while counting off seconds aloud. She developed, printed, and matted her photographs herself, never entrusting her negatives to anyone else. By 1901 she was exhibiting her studies of rural life in the local Universalist church vestry, and soon had several prestigious exhibitions in Boston and other cities.

Dorothy was devoted to her mother, and the two shuttled back and forth between Newton and Kingfield, with occasional trips to the Carolinas and the American West. Mrs. Emmons became stone deaf by 1920, and since Dorothy was the only person whose lips she could read, Dorothy's presence was necessary for any conversation.

Mrs. Emmons stayed active in her later years despite her deafness and constant worry about money. She continued to take photographs and earned a little money painting miniatures on ivory. She died in her sleep on March 18, 1937, in Newton, and was buried in the Stanley family plot in Kingfield. Her negatives and prints remained mostly in the family through years of obscurity until they were brought to light in the late 1970s, enabling us to look back with Chansonetta Stanley Emmons through the lens of her camera at an era she had felt compelled to preserve.

A little boy was encircled by the shadow of his hoop,
West New Portland, Maine, around 1910.

The "spring blossoms" under the apple trees are unidentified, but the photograph is one of a series taken in Brighton, Massachusetts, in 1896.

Hazel True fed some Barred Rock hens at the True
farm in West New Portland about 1900. Hazel, later
Mrs. Harry Newman, recalled that Mrs. Emmons
made several exposures before she finally got the
picture she wanted, including Hazel's cat, Andy.

A farmer in Kingfield, Maine, expertly directed a stream of milk at a sleek barn-cat, about 1905.

Mrs. Emmons photographed Mary Burns as she
wove rag rugs on her large floor loom, an activity
that was declining among farm women as factory-
woven rugs became ever more available. The place
was West New Portland, Maine, in about 1905.

Lucy Butts Carville (pouring the tea), her sister-in-law, Nancy J. Butts, and her brother, the Reverend Emery Butts, were frequent subjects for Mrs. Emmons' camera. This noon-day meal was photographed in West New Portland in 1902.

In 1927, Dorothy enrolled in an oil-painting class
conducted at Rockport, Massachusetts, by Aldro T.
Hibbard, a well-known artist of the time. The class
was painting a model, with the sea as a backdrop,
when Mrs. Emmons took this photograph.

This romantic photograph of Mrs. Emmons' daughter, Dorothy, at age 19 was made as she gazed out to sea from the rocks at Ogunquit, Maine, in 1910.

Three fishermen repaired lines in the waning light
of late afternoon, probably near New Bedford, Massachusetts, in the 1920s.

Three bathers at Scituate, Massachusetts, in 1908 headed out into the surf. This photograph is one of Mrs. Emmons' rare attempts to stop action and capture a moment of spontaneity, rather than to carefully orchestrate a photograph that would preserve the past instead of the present.

Acknowledgments

Many people helped create this book. Special thanks go to Ellie Reichlin of the Society for the Preservation of New England Antiquities in Boston, for her expertise and good judgment; to John Pierce, managing editor of YANKEE magazine, for help in shaping the concept of the book; to Judson Hale, editor of YANKEE; and to Sandra Taylor, Guy Russell, Sharon Smith, and Dick Heckman of Yankee Books for patient editorial support and criticism; to the staffs of the New Hampshire Historical Society, the Old Gaol Museum in York, Maine, and the Cranston (Rhode Island) Historical Society; and to Mrs. Elsie Barstow, Lorraine Moore, Chris and Helen Thurber, Marius and Mildred Péladeau, Kristie Rubendunst and Michael Mackay, and Henry Dubroff, for information, helpfulness, and much-appreciated hospitality.

S.M.

Credits

Henry Greenwood Peabody: *Page 6, Dartmouth College Library; pages 8-21, Society for the Preservation of New England Antiquities (SPNEA), Boston, Massachusetts.* Henry P. Moore: *New Hampshire Historical Society.* Emma Lewis Coleman: *SPNEA; biographical information from exhibition text prepared by Ellie Reichlin.* Baldwin Coolidge: *SPNEA; biographical information from article about Coolidge in* Old-Time New England *(Vol. LXIX, Nos. 3-4) by Ellie Reichlin.* Frederick B. Quimby: *Pages 56, 61-63, Old Gaol Museum, York, Maine; pages 58-60, 64-69, SPNEA.* Lena Osgood Long: *Saxtons River (Vermont) Historical Society; biographical information courtesy of Lorraine Moore and Mrs. Elisha Camp.* George Edward Tingley: *Photographs and biographical information courtesy of Mrs. Elsie Barstow.* Henry L. Hadcock: *SPNEA.* Warwick Stevens Carpenter: *Collection of Chris and Helen Thurber, North Bennington, Vermont; biographical information courtesy of Mildred Ledden, New York State Library, Albany.* Frederick W. Greene: *F. W. Greene Estate, Inc.; biographical information courtesy of Henry Dubroff, also Theodore P. Greene.* Wilfred E. Stone: *Pages 130, 132-135, 138-146, The Wilfred Stone Collection, in the care of Kristie Rubendunst and Michael Mackay; pages 136-137, 147, Cranston (Rhode Island) Historical Society; biographical information courtesy of Kristie Rubendunst, Michael Mackay, and Amey Rubendunst.* Chansonetta Stanley Emmons: *Pages 148, 151-156, 158-159, Emmons/Stanley Collection, owned by Marius B. Péladeau and Samuel Pennington; page 150, by permission of Charles G. Whitchurch, Wilmette, Illinois; page 157, Cutler Memorial Library, Farmington, Maine.*

Frontispiece photograph by Henry L. Hadcock.